Old Skipton

Paul Chrystal

Text © Paul Chrystal, 2020.
First published in the United Kingdom, 2020, reprinted 2025
by Stenlake Publishing Ltd.,
54-58 Mill Square,
Catrine, Ayrshire,
KA5 6RD

Telephone: 01290 551122
www.stenlake.co.uk

Printed by P2D,
1 Newlands Way,
Westoning, MK45 5LD

ISBN 9781840338881

The publishers regret that they cannot supply copies of any pictures featured in this book.

Acknowledgements

Thanks to 'Skipton Castle, Yorkshire' for permission to use the image of Conduit Court; to William and John Whitaker, Whitakers Chocolates Ltd; and to John Frankland, Outreach Librarian – West, Skipton Library and Information Centre for access to and permission to use the images from the Rowley Ellwood Collection. The Rowley Ellwood Collection is an online gallery of over 500 historic old photos of Skipton, fully indexed and searchable. These photos are available for viewing on CD or DVD at Skipton Reference Library.

The following photos are Rowley images: front cover; back cover; pages 2, 5 (lower), 6, 7, 13, 15, 17, 18, 19, 20, 21, 22, 23 (right), 24, 25, 28, 32, 33, 34 (left), 36, 37 (left) 39, 44, 48. Reproduced by kind permission of the Ellwood family, V. Rowley, and North Yorkshire County Council, Skipton Library.

Left: A Skipton lady enjoying her pipe.

Introduction

Craven: "The exact extent of it we nowhere find"
– Thomas Cox in his 1731 *Magna Britannia et Hibernia Antiqua Nova*

Skipton, a pleasant and bustling market town in the Craven district of North Yorkshire, is on the River Aire and the Leeds and Liverpool Canal at the southern edge of the Yorkshire Dales. Over the years the town has benefitted enormously from the canal, Britain's longest inland waterway at 127 miles which opened in 1816 with 96 locks along its course. The canal took 46 years to cut, and finally came in at five times the original budget. The first part to be completed was the lock-free section from Skipton to Bingley, in 1773. In the 19th century the busy canal carried stone, coal, wool, cotton, limestone, grain, and other goods. The most important cargo was always coal, with over a million tons per year being delivered to Liverpool from the Yorkshire collieries in the 1860s.

The people of Skipton were dancing in the street when the canal opened on their doorstep. *The Leeds Intelligencer* reported on 8th April 1773: "On Thursday last, that part of the Grand Canal from Bingley to Skipton was opened, and two boats laden with coals arrived at the last mentioned place, which were sold at half the price they have hitherto given for that most necessary convenience of life, which is a recent instance, among other, of the great use of canals in general. On which occasion the bells were set ringing at Skipton; there were also bonfires, illuminations, and other demonstrations of joy."

Navigation westwards from Skipton was problematic; it was finally resolved after many years by a tunnel at Foulridge in 1896. In 1906 the Leeds and Liverpool Canal carried 2,337,401 tons of cargo an average distance of 22 miles, and produced £180,000 in revenue. Skipton's population more than trebled between 1801 and 1881; the population of Skipton was 14,623 in 2011. Skipton, the name, is made up of the Old English *sceap* (sheep) and *tun* (town or village). The market, stemming from its formative years, still thrives. The town features in the *Domesday Book* of 1086; it was strategically important during the English Civil War and the site of a prisoner of war camp during the First World War. In 2016, for the second time, Skipton was voted the best place to live in England.

Right: I wish I could say that these sheep on the way to market were in Sheep Street, outside the Wooly Sheep pub; but I can't – they are, of course, flocking from the Railway Inn in Cavendish Street, on October 11 1944.

Skipton Castle was built in 1090 as a classic wooden motte-and-bailey by Norman baron Robert de Romille, lord of the estates of Bolton Abbey, very soon after the Conquest. In the 12th century William le Gros fortified it with a stone keep to repel attacks from the marauding Scots; this had the significant effect of elevating Skipton from a lowly village to a burgh administered by a reeve. The security and protection afforded by Skipton Castle during the Middle Ages encouraged the urbanisation of the surrounding area, and during times of war and disorder the town acted as a magnet drawing in families. It remains one of the most complete and best preserved medieval castles in England. The wording above the gateway – *désormais* – means 'henceforth', nothing if not optimistic for the future.

The castle (under the command of Sir John Mallory) was the last remaining Royalist stronghold in the north of England until its surrender on 20th December 1645 after a three-year siege; elmwood pipes brought water from outside, but when the castle was besieged and the pipeline cut off, the inhabitants depended on rainwater collected from the roof and channelled into a cistern beneath the Conduit Court. A well was uncovered recently, helping to explain how the castle garrison survived the siege for so long. Lady Anne Clifford (1590–1676) was the last Clifford to own it. After the siege, she ordered repairs and planted a yew tree in the central courtyard in 1659 to commemorate its restoration; the yew is still there. The castle is the start of the 100-mile Lady Anne's Way long distance path to Penrith.

The museum was founded on 6th October 1928 by a group of enthusiasts drawn from local groups such as the Craven Naturalists and Scientific Association, Skipton Mechanics' Institute, Friends Adult School and the Workers' Educational Association and was initially housed in the library. The aim was to house a number of existing collections including the finds from the Elbolton Cave excavations, the Craven Herbarium and Richard Tiddeman's reef knoll collection. A few of the many collections on display include: *Archaeology* – finds range from the Paleolithic to post-medieval many of which have been found on local excavations. Collections include cave finds from nearby Elbolton and Victoria Caves, a lithics collection, finds from Doggerbank, Roman finds from nearby Kirk Sink Villa and from the Sunderland collection, and an Elizabethan coin hoard. An incomplete copy of Shakespeare's First Folio owned by a local businessman and donated by his daughter in the 1930s is one of only four on display in the world; *Mouseman Collection* – a collection of 17 objects made by Robert Thompson; *Amethyst Intaglio* – a Roman engraved amethyst found in nearby Hellifield and donated to the museum in 1934. The carving depicts a man, probably Odysseus, offering wine to the cyclops Polyphemus before blinding him. Intaglios were used to make seals by stamping the intaglio in wax.

Caroline Square just off Keighley Road in the 1940s when this was home to Skipton's bus station. On Friday 16th May 2014 at 9.15pm, after 88 years the last of the distinctive orange and black buses of Pennine Motor Services bus pulled out Stand 3 at Skipton Bus Station to make the final journey to Settle, the end of an era in Yorkshire transport history. The company had been founded in 1925 by brothers Arthur and Vic Simpson, who owned and ran a garage, and their brother-in-law Jim Windle. Their first bus, a new 14-seat char-a-banc built by the Overland company, ran from Skipton High Street on Christmas Eve morning with only three passengers on board on the entire journey, and by the time it got to Settle it was empty (apart from the driver and conductor).

Looking down the High Street from the church tower, *c*.1930. The High Street is home to the famous Skipton Market which today dominates the town four days a week. Its success was boosted by the opening of the Leeds-Liverpool Canal in 1774. The town stocks were near the old Tolbooth as were the cells for felons. The market's history dates back to medieval times, when a Royal Charter from King John (r.1199–1216) granted to 'The Lord of the Honour' (the owner) of Skipton Castle to hold a fair on Skipton High Street. Every market day, stalls are erected on the area of the High Street known as the "setts" – areas between the formal footpaths and the main road. There are no fixed stalls. Traders bring their own – and they are built and dismantled at the start and the end of each market day.

Possibly the earliest known photograph of Skipton: the High Street's other claim to fame is Skipton Show where the town's dependence on agriculture, particularly sheep, was shown each year. Skipton Show, also known as the Craven Agricultural Show was held from 1855 to 1929. The shop near left was Scott the tubmaker which existed from 1822 to 1884 – his tubs were for butter. Another major High Street event is the annual Skipton Sheep Day which showcases what Skipton and the Yorkshire Dales have to offer.

In 1903 Skipton asked Andrew Carnegie for £6,000 to establish a library, but received only £3,000 – a penny rate would have to be levied for the purchase of books, as well as extra funds raised to liquidate the mortgages on the two shops which stood on the proposed site. By 1906 the conditions were met and the Carnegie funds granted. The library finally opened in 1910. The public reading room was on the ground floor, and upstairs was split into a reference library and a lending library, with about 7,000 books available to borrow, as well as a separate children's library. In 1914 the Petyt Library – consisting of 2,500 volumes of 17th century recusant literature was bequeathed by Sylvester Petyt to the library. By 2018 the collection was taking up space needed for IT equipment. York University library, hearing of this, decided to digitise the collection and it was moved there.

Skipton brothers William and Sylvester Petyt had moved to London from their native Skipton in the mid-1600s, to pursue careers in law. Mindful of the education that Skipton had given them the brothers began creating a library, shipping the books back to Skipton creating what's now known as 'The Petyt Collection'. Recusant literature is literature in breach of the Act of Uniformity of 1559, written by those who refused to attend Anglican services; in other words, religious works by English Catholics.

Skipton Railway Station 1905. Skipton's first station was opened on 7th September 1847 by the Leeds and Bradford Extension Railway, as a temporary terminus of its line from Bradford. The line was extended to Colne a year later. Initially, passengers would get off the train at Skipton for onward travel to the villages of Wharfedale by horse-drawn coach. In 1849 the "little" North Western Railway opened a line from Skipton to Ingleton, eventually extending to Lancaster and Morecambe in 1850. On 30th April 1876, Skipton Station was relocated a quarter of a mile to the northwest; by this time both the Leeds and Bradford and North Western Railways had been absorbed by the Midland Railway. The new station coincided with the opening of the Midland's Settle-Carlisle Line, which made Skipton a station on the London St. Pancras to Glasgow main line. On 1st October 1888 platforms 5 and 6 were added to serve the Skipton to Ilkley Line. They were also later used by the Yorkshire Dales Railway, a short branch to Grassington, from 1902 to 1930.

Managers and staff at Skipton Railway Station in the 1930s with the engine shed in the background. The handling of freight and passenger services was a major and vital operation (often forgotten) in town and cities, ports, coal mines and factories servicing the myriad lines that criss-crossed the country. There were numerous 'sheds' spread throughout the length and breadth of the UK that furnished and serviced the army of steam locomotives of which there were 20,000 by 1948.

The Thames-Clyde Express' entering Skipton Station in 1961. Leaving London St. Pancras at 10.15 it would reach Glasgow St. Enoch via Carlisle and Dumfries at 19.45. Here it is pulled by BR Britannia Pacific No. 70044 *Earl Haig*. In the distance are Skipton Moor and Rombalds Moor.

The Infectious Diseases Hospital opened in Skipton in 1902, providing effective isolation for the whole Skipton urban district. Before that there had only been a temporary building with just 12 beds. The new 42-bed hospital was built on Cawder Hill at a cost of £16,000. Airedale General Hospital opened in July 1970, subsuming a number of smaller hospitals including Bingley Hospital; Keighley Victoria Hospital; St. John's Hospital, Keighley (a maternity hospital); and Morton Banks Hospital, which was the Keighley Infectious Diseases Hospital. There were three hospitals in Skipton – Cawder Ghyll (a maternity hospital), Skipton General, and Raikeswood. There was also Castle Hill Hospital at Settle.

Union Square off Broughton Road. Built in the early 1800s the top storeys were given over to hand loom weaving as they were the best lit. The outer walls formed the supports of Union Workhouse. Skipton, as most towns, had many slum dwellings with poor sanitation, overcrowding and damp. Presumably this was taken on a Monday, if the washing is anything to go by. An Old Union Square still exists in Skipton.

Skipton War Memorial commemorates the 371 Skipton men who lost their lives in the First World War and the 76 who fell in the Second World War. The monument was unveiled on 8th April 1922. The triangular limestone pillar, about 20 feet high, carries the figure of the Greek goddess Nike (Victory). At the base is the sculpture of a naked man breaking a sword over his knee. On the front of the railings is a bronze sword with the Yorkshire rose on the hilt. There is an animal's head in relief at the top of the blade nearest the hilt. The regiments with the most fatalities are the West Riding Regiment (The Duke of Wellington's Regiment, West Riding) and the West Yorkshire Regiment. The 2nd Battalion of the DWR landed at Le Havre as part of the 13th Brigade in the 5th Division in August 1914 for service on the Western Front and first saw action at the Battle of Mons. The West Yorkshire Regiment (Prince of Wales's Own) 1st Battalion landed at Saint-Nazaire as part of the 18th Brigade in the 6th Division in September 1914. The 2nd Battalion landed at Le Havre as part of the 23rd Brigade in the 8th Division in November 1914.

Tom Clarke of the Green Howards was wounded on 11th March 1915 at Neuve Chapelle in France and died on 19th March at Netley Military Hospital aged 24. He was the eldest son of a family of sixteen of Thomas Henry and Pricilla Clarke of 20 Byron Street. The picture shows the cortege leaving Byron Street for a service at Christ Church. The youngest son Ernie was killed in action 1st March 1917 aged 19 years.

The street is home to the Wooly Sheep Inn (at No. 38) and gets its name, like the pub, from the sheep market. Sheep Street claims to be one of the most haunted streets in Yorkshire and the Wooly Sheep appears to be the centre of the hauntings. Room No.3 is a place where people fear to tread. One story goes how a man had gone down to change the barrels in the cellar. When he switched on the light he was astonished to see a woman in the far corner, as startled to see him as he was of her. She was dressed in a billowing pink ball gown so he assumed she was a guest who had lost her way, maybe searching for the toilets. But then he saw that her legs went right through the floor! He couldn't have known that renovations had taken place and a new floor had been laid six inches above the previous one. He packed up and left soon afterwards, but the pink lady has been seen in the cellar many times since.

The High Street in the 1940s with an impressive array of motor cars, and Holy Trinity Church in the background. Some award-winning ice cream to be had at the kiosk, with diplomas won at Crystal Palace and Olympia. The posh cars indicate a reasonable level of affluence in some of the townsfolk and people from the country around the town. Wendy's café is on the left.

On Saturday 13th July 1901, a gala was held on the Brick Buildings Fields off Bailey Road to raise money for the Skipton and District Cottage Hospital, built at the time of Queen Victoria's Jubilee. Extra trains were put on to bring visitors in from miles around. After the formation of the National Health Service in July 1948, the Skipton Charities Gala continued raising money for local charities and non-profit-making organisations. The gala, held every year on the second Saturday in June, starts with a procession through the town centre to Aireville Park, where numerous performance acts entertain the public, culminating in live music and a firework display. This float, outside The Devonshire Hotel, Newmarket Street, refers to the *Terra Nova* Expedition (officially the British Antarctic Expedition). This expedition to Antarctica, between 1910 and 1913, was led by Robert Falcon Scott who wanted to be the first person to reach the geographic South Pole. He and four companions reached it on 17th January 1912, but found that the Norwegian team led by Roald Amundsen had beaten them by 34 days. Scott's entire party died on the return journey.

'Royalists seeking refuge in the house of a Puritan'. A brilliant float from 1916, inspired by an engraving of the same name by J.D. Cooper RA (fl. 1860). An obvious reference to the English Civil War.

The Independent Order of Rechabites also known as the Sons and Daughters of Rechab, was a fraternal organisation and friendly society founded in 1835 as part of the wider temperance movement to promote total abstinence from alcohol. It was founded as the Salford Unity of Rechabites, in Salford. Their first lodge was "Tent Ebenezer #1" and soon "tents" were founded for adult females (over the age of 12), boys (aged 12-16), and for children of both sexes (age 5-12), as well as other adult males (age 16 and up).

Skipton and District Warp Dressers Association, winners of the Overdale Shield at the Hospital Gala in 1909. According to the Rowley Collection the photograph was taken at the rear of the Firth Shed Manager's House, Skipton with Upper Sackville Street in the background. The Warp Dressers Association was a trade union representing workers involved in preparing warp yarn for weaving; unusually for a textile union, it embraced workers in a variety of materials, including cotton, wool and worsted. It was also unusual in that it did not provide any support for industrial action, but instead saw its principal purpose as an employment exchange. The Skipton & District Association was formed in 1891, had 200 or so members and was dissolved in 1920.

Christ Church Schools Pierrots – Hospital Gala 1903. In the days before you could easily smile for the camera. A pierrot is a stock character in pantomime and commedia dell'arte whose origins are in the late 17th-century Italian troupes of players performing in Paris and known as the Comédie-Italienne; the name is a diminutive of Pierre with the suffix -ot. Pantomime apart, the pierrot was very popular in fetes and carnivals up and down the UK, particularly in seaside resorts. In the 20th century they were usurped by the English clown.

Left: Meet Berry and Matt, instructor and door keeper at the Skipton Roller Skating Rink. Ella Hatfield writes in *Skipton* (1991): "Skipton also had a skating rink, on Broughton Road, whose directors reserved the right to refuse admission to 'any person who may appear to be undesirable'…the skating rink was later destroyed by fire, and there was another, smaller one for a time at the bottom of Raikes Road." Joyce Murgatroyd writes in *Growing Up In Old Skipton* (2011), 'one day my brother announced that a roller skating rink had been started in the Temperance Hall…this became popular, and before long a large wooden building was erected where now the timber yard stands [now Magnet and Kwik Fit]…here we spent many hours clinging to the rails, or to an instructor, until we learnt to do the most complicated steps and dances."

Right: Raikeswood Camp, in the north-west of Skipton at what is now Salisbury Street, was built in early 1915 as a military training camp for the Bradford Pals (16th Battalion West Yorkshire Regiment) and was subsequently used by a number of other regiments, including the Leeds Bantams (17th Battalion West Yorkshire Regiment) and the Black Watch. From January 1918, it was used as a prisoner-of-war camp holding some 500 officers and 130 soldiers. The camp was operational until October 1919. Following the discovery of a book in Skipton library written by a group of German officers during their time in Skipton, work began on a translation, entitled Kriegsgefangen in Skipton. Overdale Camp (later Overdale Caravan Park) was used as a POW camp during the Second World War, holding both Italians and Germans.

Terrified children from Wesley Higher Grade School in 1902. The English higher grade schools formed a key part of an expanding 19th-century education system, but they threatened the vested interests of a powerful establishment intent on maintaining the status quo. They were seen as competition to the traditional schools and undesirable particularly as they emphasised scientific, technical and vocational education.

Skipton Urban District Council Fire Brigade, with fire engine, on Lower Commercial Street in 1924. *Back row, left to right*: Bill Robinson (driver), Arthur Hudson, Jack Webster, David Pickles (peaked cap) who worked at Dewhurst's and was in charge of the fire engine. *Front row, left to right*: Percy Field (?), Ernest Thornton, Alfred Anderton, Jack Nutter, Billy Friend.

Park Shed Mill Workers. Skipton's position on the Leeds and Liverpool Canal made it an ideal location for mills. Built in 1889 by Thomas Wilkinson, and just as often known as Wilkinson's, Mill Park Shed Mill is unusual in that it is the only mill in Skipton not to be built right next to the canal presumably because the other seven Skipton mills occupied the available space. It is on the corner of Shortbank Road and Brougham Street. The other seven are: Belle Vue Mills; Broughton Road Shed; Firth Sheds; High Mill; Low Mill; Union Mills and Victoria Mill.

Park Shed – best decorated mill for what may have been Queen Victoria's Golden Jubilee in 1887. But it wasn't all fun and games or unalloyed patriotism. The nature of work changed completely during the Industrial Revolution from a cottage industry model to a factory-centric model. In England and Scotland in 1788, two-thirds of the workers in 143 water-powered cotton mills were children. Sir Robert Peel, a mill owner turned reformer, promoted the 1802 'Health and Morals of Apprentices Act', which was intended to stop pauper children having to work more than 12 hours a day in mills. Children typically started in the mills at around the age of four, working as mule scavengers under the working machinery until age eight. They then graduated to working as little piecers until age fifteen, working 14 to 16 hours a day, and flogged if they fell asleep. The children were drafted to the mills of Derbyshire, Yorkshire and Lancashire from workhouses in London and other towns in southern England. Most of the adult workers in cotton factories in mid-19th century Britain had begun their work as child labourers.

Group of Spinners High Mill, Skipton Woods 1868.

Other Skipton mills include: **High Mill** – the first industrial mill built in Skipton in 1785 at the entrance to Skipton Woods; it was a cotton spinning mill powered by water. In 1825 an annex was added with steam power. **Low Mill / Sackville Mill** – built in 1839 for weft spinning and weaving, on Sackville Street became known as the Silk Mill after its sale in 1892 and was employed in silk making. The mill burned down in 1908, resulting in the loss of 300 local jobs. A new mill called Sackville Mill was erected on the same site. **Firth Shed** – built 1877, housing 300 looms was extended in 1906 to add another 200 looms. It made dyed cotton goods and winceys. **Victoria Mill** – owned by International Textile Co Ltd. **Union Mill** – a cotton weaving mill, built 1867 by Skipton Land & Building Company, run by Skipton Mill Co Ltd. 800 looms manufacturing winceys, stripes and checks. Steam-powered, one-storey shed with attached warehouse. Extension added 1872, dyehouse added 1875. **Broughton Road Mill** – built 1897 by the Skipton Room and Power Co Ltd. Burned down 1958. **Alexandra Mill** – On Keighley Road, Skipton, built 1887 by George Walton, with a weaving shed holding 500 looms, manufacturing dress goods, skirtings and shirtings. Later taken over by Walton Hainsworth and Co.

AIREDALE MILL FIRE. MARCH 31 1906.

Mills had a habit of bursting into flames and being destroyed by fire because of the dust and fibres blowing around in them. Airedale Mill was at Kildwick, Skipton. In March 1906 fire tore through the mill only three months after an inferno at Farnhill Mill which was situated almost directly opposite Airedale Mill, on the other side of the canal and main Keighley to Skipton road. About 100 workers would lose their jobs and the mill would have to be pulled down, the *Craven Herald* reported, praising the efforts of the Skipton brigade "once a cause for derision". The alarm was given at 10.24pm, the engine left Coach Street at 10.30, was at the scene at 10.50 and at 11pm was taking water from the River Aire. The Keighley brigade, summoned at the same time, arrived 25 minutes after the Skipton men even though by seven minutes past midnight both the Skipton and Keighley Fire Brigades had been notified. However, although the Skipton brigade responded immediately, the Keighley brigade declined to turn out, their reason being that Farnhill was outside the area normally covered by the Keighley brigade and, as no payment had been made by the owners of the mill towards the upkeep of the Keighley service, they were not required to attend. Unfortunately, the central section of the roof had collapsed before either of them arrived; and before they could get to work the whole of the building was fully alight and beyond saving. This photograph, taken by the Farnhill photographer George Whiteoak, shows the crowd gathered on the Keighley Road to view the ruins of Airedale Mill.

This shows the devastation caused by a fire at the Silk Mill, in Sackville Street, Skipton, in November 1908. The mill, originally known as Low Mill, was built in 1839 by John Benson Sidgwick for spinning and weaving yarns, but had become known as Silk Mill after being bought in 1892 by Rickard's of Airton, who then used it for silk-making. The 1908 blaze resulted in the loss of 300 jobs in the town – where, of course, there was little or no formal social security provision.

The Midland Hotel in the 1920s, now Herriots Hotel, on Broughton Road with Belle Vue Mills in the background. Belle Vue Mills, or Dewhurst's, was built in 1828 as a spinning and weaving mill, but burned down two years later, and was immediately rebuilt; in 1852 an extension was added to allow for another 385 looms. In 1882 the mill had a floor area of 20,000 square yards spread over five storeys, and employed over 800 workers. In 1886 electric lighting was installed. The Belle Vue Mills did spinning, weaving, making of sewing cotton (Sylko) and dyeing. The hotel is a fairly typical late 19th century railway hotel built by the Midland Railway Company.

Dobson's was on the High Street, next to the town hall on the corner of the road leading to Jerry Croft ginnel. Tooth extractions were available here for one shilling. The building later became Whitaker's: one door led up to the main kitchen on the first floor and the other to a small workman's café on the ground floor. The main dining room was above, and accessed from inside the shop. Local pharmaceutical competition came in the form of Brown's the Chemist.

Manby's garage on Lower Union Street. There was also a Fred Manby & Bros ironmongers-cum-gunsmith with its famous illuminated clock installed May 20th 1912. Manby's closed in 1986 after about 170 years trading. Other items for sale included those semi-circular steel dog whistles that the dales farmers used, tools and every size of screw and nail imaginable. Even if you bought one nail it was wrapped up for you.

G. Sutherland – fish, fruit and poultry in Sheep Street.

Abram's Middle Row Garage in the High Street.

H.O. Walker, Bootmaker & Co., Keighley Road; later run by the Meakin Brothers. The building on the left by the lamppost at the start of Waller Hill was a gents urinal. You can see the beck which now flows under Sunwin House on the right where it emerges from under the road and the shoe shop. On the opposite side of the road (to the left of the camera) was the road leading down to the stepping stones. The shop closed in June 1979 as it was flooded in the great inundation of that year, soon before the owners were due to retire. Walker's kept the shoe lasts for the local gentry. The girl in the picture is Evelyn Hall; she used to walk the 2.3 miles into Skipton from Carleton – and back.

J. Metcalfe, auctioneers and furniture showroom on Sheep Street Hill. Other auctioneers in 1837 included Thomas Edmondson in Chancery Lane and Garnetts in High Street.

The New Ship 1914. Margaret Alderson, Jack Alderson?, Fred Alderson, Tom Pickles, Charlie Baldwin, Tom Clarke – gamekeeper at Skipton Castle returning from a successful foxhunt.

H. Lister – newsagent, Keighley Road. *The Daily Sketch* was running a story about Kitchener going to Egypt. Herbert Kitchener (1850–1916, Field Marshal Horatio Herbert Kitchener, 1st Earl Kitchener) was an Army officer and colonial administrator famous for his role in the First World War but notorious for his imperial campaigns, most especially his scorched earth policy against the Boers and his establishment of concentration camps during the Second Boer War in which between 18,000 and 28,000 men, women and children died, mainly from disease. The headline probably refers to June 1911 when Kitchener returned to Egypt as British Agent and Consul-General in Egypt.

G.H. Mason & Sons – telephone engineers around 1932. Note the early microphone. Their shop was on the site of the Old Black Bull Inn, later the Sun Inn. In 1928 it, along with Phillips the butcher next door were demolished and a new G.H. Masons built.

Draymen and lorry, delivering in Skipton. Timothy Taylor's is a family-owned brewery founded in 1858 in Keighley by Timothy Taylor. Their best-known ale is Landlord, a pale ale which was created for miners, to compete against local rival Barnsley Bitter. The brand grew in popularity in 2003 when Madonna said in an interview that it was her favourite beer.

Shell-Mex was one of the leading UK petrol brands. Shell-Mex and BP Ltd was a British joint marketing venture between Royal Dutch Shell (Shell) and British Petroleum (BP). It was formed in 1932 when both companies decided to merge their United Kingdom marketing operations, partly in response to the difficult economic conditions. The garage could also boast some prestigious marques.

Outside the Hole I' Th' Wall on the High Street in a charabanc. Also later called Chew's Bar; there was a pub on this site up until the mid 1970s: in 1976 the pub was closing and Skipton Building Society rented the upper floors as office space whilst the building now known as Providence Quarter was being built as their head office. Now a shop. Here are some other closed Skipton pubs: Commercial, 38 Water Street; Craven Arms, 12 Newmarket Street; Lock Stock & Barrel, Coach Street; Royal Oak, 2 Water Street; Ship, Gargrave Road; Snaygill Arms, Keighley Road.

Skipton Amateur Swimming Club 1911. Comments from the Rowley Collection website: 'The men and youths in this photo didn't know it when it was taken but they were to bear the brunt of two World Wars. Those who survived would have been in their fifties and sixties when I started swimming here. They are gathered in the shallow end where, if I remember correctly, there was a short flight of step in the corner. A simple diving platform can be seen on the left and further to the left, in the middle of the end wall was a foot bath and a long flight of concrete steps leading up to the open air pool, which was a converted reservoir. At the other end was the high diving board which reached almost to the roof. The changing cubicles, as can be seen behind the man with the towel, were half doors and pretty cramped. We went as often as we could afford and sometimes with the school for swimming lessons, even though nearly everyone I knew could swim already.' Added by: Peter Sheeran 14th Aug 2006.

'At these baths I learnt to swim, I would have been about 5 (1953) we went as much as we could afford to go during the summer holidays not sure but I think it cost us 3d; the shallow end was 3ft 6ins and the deep end 5ft 4ins.' Added by: Lynda Marley (Nee Crayden) 24th July 2008.

Men of Trinity Methodist Church serving teas, dressed appropriately, in the 1920s.

Skipton Church gathering.

Skipton Baptist Chapel village play.

Skipton Comic Band

Queen Victoria's Jubilee 1887. Their expressions say it all. Taken at the back of Brick Hall Inn, now the Woolly Sheep. The building in the background was the workshop of Charlie Mathers Jnr, carpenter and undertaker. Handy for the ox. One of the most enduring events of the 1887 Jubilee was the building of the Farnhill Pinnacle; it has been an unmissable landmark on the landscape ever since. As well as the ox feast, the people of Kildwick and Farnhill wanted to mark the occasion with a lasting reminder of the event; the decision was, therefore, taken to rebuild the cairn on Farnhill Crag which had been placed there by J.R. Tenant Esq of Kildwick Hall around 1857 but had since fallen into disrepair. A wooden box was placed inside the cairn containing various artefacts. Kildwick stonemason Robert Tillotson inscribed the letters V.R.1837-87 on a large stone to the south east of the Pinnacle.

Jim Stanford's butchers have been established for over 80 years; for all that time they have kept to the same recipes and traditional ways of making their famous pies, sausage and other quality products. Pork, lamb and beef cuts are bought directly from the Auction Mart where they have a state of the art cutting plant. Sheep and cattle apart, auctions for sheepdogs are also held at Skipton. The world record price was broken in 2011 with £6,300 for Dewi Fan and again in May 2016, when Cap was sold at Skipton for £16,000.

This charabanc left the road at Blacko, near Barrowford, and crashed into an old Toll Bar House on the Gisburn Road. Two of the men, seated at the back, died instantly when they were thrown out of the vehicle into the toll house. Three others died soon afterwards from their injuries. It was just a regular day out: the motorbus with fifteen passengers had set off from Grassington before lunchtime picking up more passengers in Skipton; there had been the usual stops at hotels when at about 2pm the charabanc, having just left the Moorcock Inn, attempted a sharp bend, left the road and smacked into the toll bar house. The men, who died at the scene, including one who died as he was being put onto a stretcher, were taken to the Cross Keys Inn in Blacko, while the injured were taken to Nelson's Reedyford Hospital. The next day multitudes of ghoulish people drove to the scene to gawp at the mangled vehicle. The charabanc driver, Frank Bailey, from Burnsall, was arrested and charged with being drunk in charge of a vehicle and with manslaughter. He first appeared at Colne Magistrates' Court and was sent to Manchester Assizes for trial. In February 1921 'he was acquitted after a doctor who examined him at Barrowford Police Station declared him not drunk at all, but perfectly sober and that his demeanour immediately following the accident had been of shock and not of drunkenness'. 'Bailey had told an earlier inquest that when the charabanc had arrived in Skipton, he had drunk a small whisky at the King's Arms. He stopped again in Gisburn, where he had drunk another small whisky, and had then driven on to Barrowford, where at lunchtime he had drunk a third small whisky and bought a packet of cigarettes and a cigar'.

Embsay Moor Reservoir – opening day June 21st 1910. Monika Butler has undertaken detailed research into Skipton's water supply down the ages. This owes much to her work which appeared in the *Craven Herald* 23rd January 2010: 'The reservoir that brought water to the masses': She tells how in the 19th century 'there was no continuous supply of clean water to Skipton. The first attempt to harness water from the surrounding hills rather than relying on wells had been made in 1765, when the Earl of Thanet… harnessed the spring water rising around the present Shortbank Road and bring it into town in pipes. For this privilege, the lessees had to pay every year at "the common dining hall of the castle of Skipton, the rent or sum of one pound of lawful money of Great Britain". Standpipes were erected for use by the public at the Town Hall steps in Sheep Street, at the Market Cross, at Bunkers Hill and Mill Bridge, and in August 1824 a pipe was laid into Union Square'. Fast forward to 1910 and the Embsay Moor Reservoir was complete: and the 'dam was watertight, the reservoir began to fill and on January 10th 1910 had attained the full volume of more than 175,000,000 gallons'. On June 21st 1910, Councillor WRG Farey JP officially opened the reservoir by operating a valve in the valve tower, allowing water to flow into Skipton's main supply. Councillor Farey was presented with a gold key for the valve tower which can still be seen at Craven Museum.

The Old Tithe Barn in Swadford Street. The slate roof replaced a thatch in 1750. In its latter years it was the haunt of salesmen, travelling troupes and theatre companies as a kind of ad hoc theatre venue. In 1901 it became Stockdale's Wine & Spirit Lodge.